**A Timeline of
Space Exploration**

Stargazing to Space
Travel

WORLD
BOOK

World Book
a Scott Fetzer company
Chicago

World Book, Inc.
180 North LaSalle Street
Suite 900
Chicago, Illinois 60601
USA

For information about other World Book publications, call
1-800-WORLDBK (967-5325).

For information about sales to schools and libraries, call 1-800-975-3250 (United States) or 1-800-837-5365 (Canada).

Produced for World Book, Inc. by Bailey Publishing Associates Ltd.

Library of Congress Cataloging-in-Publication Data

Title: Stargazing to space travel: a timeline of space exploration.
Description: Chicago: World Book, Inc., a Scott Fetzer company, 2016. | Series: A timeline of ... | Includes index.
Identifiers: LCCN 2016012918 | ISBN 9780716635451
Subjects: LCSH: Astronomy--History--Juvenile literature. | Outer space--Exploration--Juvenile literature.
Classification: LCC QB46 .S88 2016 | DDC 520.9--dc23
LC record available at https://lccn.loc.gov/2016012918

Stargazing to Space Travel: A Timeline of Space Exploration
ISBN: 978-0-7166-3545-1
A Timeline of... Set ISBN: 978-0-7166-3539-0
E-book ISBN: 978-0-7166-3554-3 (ePUB3 format)

Printed in China by Shenzhen Wing King Tong Paper Products Co., Ltd., Guangdong Province
1st printing July 2016

Acknowledgments

Cover photo: Shutterstock (Hein Nouwens).

Bridgeman 6 (Ashmolean Museum, University of Oxford), 7 (De Agostini), 12 (Philip Mould), 13 left (National Geographic Creative).

Corbis 8 (Enzo & Paolo Ragazzini), 10 left (National Geographic Creative), 10 right (Stapleton Collection), 11 (National Geographic Creative), 14 right (Hulton-Deutsch Collection), 17 right (Bettmann), 18 right (Bettmann), 24 (NASA-digital version copyright/Science Faction), 25, 29 (Roger Ressmeyer), 30 left.

Getty 4 top (Ann Ronan Pictures), 9 (Werner Forman), 15 (Universal Images Group), 16 (MPI), 17 left (Margaret Bourke-White), 19 (Ralph Morse), 20 right (Sovfoto), 21 (Ludek Pesek), 22 right (Interim Archives), 28 right (STR/AFP), 34 left, 34 right (Akihiro IKESHITA/AFP).

NASA 4 bottom (JPL-Caltech/MSSS), 13 right (JPL-Caltech), 14 left (JPL-Caltech/UCLA/MPS/DLR/IDA/Justin Cowart), 18 left, 20 left, 22 left, 23 (JPL), 26, 27, 28 left (ESA/G. Bacon (STScI)), 30 right, 31, 32, 33 (JPL/Space Science Institute), 35 (Tim Pyle), 36 (JPL-Caltech/MSSS), 37 (JHUAPL/SwRI).

Staff

Writer: Alex Woolf

Executive Committee

President
Jim O'Rourke

Vice President and Editor in Chief
Paul A. Kobasa

Vice President, Finance
Donald D. Keller

Vice President, Marketing
Jean Lin

Vice President, International
Kristin Norell

Director, Human Resources
Bev Ecker

Editorial

Manager, Annuals/Series Nonfiction
Christine Sullivan

Editor, Annuals/Series Nonfiction
Kendra Muntz

Manager, Sciences
Jeff De La Rosa

Researcher, Sciences
Will Adams

Administrative Assistant Annuals/Series Nonfiction
Ethel Matthews

Manager, Contracts & Compliance (Rights & Permissions)
Loranne K. Shields

Manager, Indexing Services
David Pofelski

Digital

Director, Digital Product Content Development
Emily Kline

Director, Digital Product Development
Erika Meller

Digital Product Manager
Lyndsie Manusos

Digital Product Coordinator
Matthew Werner

Manufacturing/Production

Manufacturing Manager
Sandra Johnson

Production/Technology Manager
Anne Fritzinger

Proofreader
Nathalie Strassheim

Graphics and Design

Senior Art Director
Tom Evans

Senior Designer
Matt Carrington

Media Editor
Rosalia Bledsoe

Manager, Cartographic Services
Wayne K. Pichler

Senior Cartographer
John M. Rejba

Special thanks to:

Roberta Bailey
Nicola Barber
Ian Winton
Alex Woolf

Glossary There is a glossary of terms on page 38. Terms defined in the glossary are in type that **looks like this** (called *boldface type*) on their first appearance on any *spread* (two facing pages).

Circa Some dates are written with *c.* before the year. The *c.* stands for *circa*. Circa means *approximately.* For example, with c. 250 B.C., the phrase is read as "circa 250 B.C.," meaning *approximately 250 B.C.* Circa can be used with both B.C. and A.D. dates.

Contents

Stargazing to Space Travel
A Timeline of Space Exploration

Ancient Greek astronomer Ptolemy (A.D. 100-165) observed the moon and stars in the A.D. 100's.

In January 2015, NASA's Curiosity **rover** took a self-portrait photo while exploring the surface of Mars.

Introduction
Space Exploration Through the Ages

When we look into the sky during the day or at night, we look into space. Space is the unending, nearly empty regions that spread out in every direction beyond Earth. People have been fascinated by the sky—space—for centuries. In fact, astronomy, the study of all of space, or the universe, is one of the oldest branches of knowledge. People in ancient civilizations created calendars, steered ships, and tried to tell what would happen in the future based on the motions of the stars and planets.

Scholars today believe the ancient Greeks were the first people to study the skies in a way that could be called *scientific*. Their ideas were mostly based on the belief that all heavenly bodies, or natural objects in space, moved around a motionless Earth. They thought that Earth lay at the center of the universe. During the Renaissance, the invention of the telescope gave scientists a more accurate understanding of space. As telescopes became more powerful, **astronomers** discovered new planets and other bodies in our **solar system** and beyond. They learned that the sun is just one of billions of stars in our **galaxy,** the Milky Way.

In the mid-1900's, advances in technology allowed people to send spacecraft into space. Since the 1960's, people have *orbited* (circled Earth), landed on the moon, and lived on board space stations. Robotic **probes** have explored the solar system and sent back extraordinary close-up images of planets, moons, **asteroids, comets,** and the sun. New discoveries continue to improve our understanding of the vast universe around Earth.

To learn more, follow the timeline through this book to trace the history of astronomy and space exploration from the earliest civilizations to the present day.

Chapter 1

Early Astronomers
c. 1300 B.C.—c. A.D. 850

Ancient civilizations observed how heavenly bodies moved in the sky in regular patterns. Farmers in ancient Egypt knew when to plant crops based upon when certain stars first appeared in the sky. The Polynesians used stars as a guide to navigate between islands in the Pacific Ocean. Early **astronomers** believed that the sun, moon, planets, and stars moved around a motionless Earth. In the 300's B.C., Greek philosopher Aristotle claimed that Earth was surrounded by 55 rotating spheres of increasing size. The invisible spheres carried the sun, moon, and the five known planets, Mercury, Venus, Mars, Jupiter, and Saturn.

During the Shang Dynasty (c. 1766 B.C.-c. 1045 B.C.) in China, astronomers named stars and charted their positions.

Babylonians living in Mesopotamia, in what is now Iraq, charted positions of bodies in space. Scribes, or writers, watched the sky every night and recorded their observations on clay tablets (below). They noted the positions of the planets in relation to the stars. Scribes also wrote about the planets' patterns of movement in the sky that repeated in different years or decades. By recording these patterns, called *cycles*, the Babylonians became skilled at predicting planetary behavior.

c. 1300 B.C.

700 B.C.

The outermost sphere carried the stars. The word *planet* comes from the Greek word *wanderer*. The Greeks thought the planets were "wandering stars." Their wanderings were a source of mystery long before Aristotle's theories.

Aristotle's theory could not explain why the planets sometimes appeared to move in irregular ways. For most of the year, the planets moved from west to east, relative to the stars. But each planet seemed to change course for part of the year, appearing to slow down, stop, and reverse direction, moving from east to west. After some days or months, the planet would appear to slow down again, stop, and return back to its eastward motion. Astronomers continued to struggle with how to take this seeming change in direction, called **retrograde motion,** into account in models of the solar system.

Greek mathematician and astronomer Eudoxus of Cnidus (395? B.C.-337? B.C.) was the first person to apply the mathematical principles of geometry to astronomy. He suggested that 27 spheres revolved around Earth. He thought that the sun and other bodies moved along these spheres. Aristotle was greatly influenced by Eudoxus's work.

370 B.C. **c. 335 B.C.**

c. 500 B.C.

Greek philosopher and mathematician Pythagoras (580? B.C.-?) argued that Earth is a *sphere* (a solid figure shaped like a ball). But some ancient peoples believed Earth was flat.

Greek philosopher Aristotle (384 B.C.-322 B.C.) studied Earth and other bodies in the sky. He used lunar **eclipses** to prove that Earth was a spherical shape. In a lunar eclipse, the moon is positioned in line with Earth and the sun. Earth's round shadow passes across the moon's surface. In time, people started to believe Earth actually was round.

Early Astronomers
c. 1300 B.C.—c. A.D. 850

Detailed astronomical records were made in China around 200 B.C. The Chinese watched and recorded such sky happenings as **comets** and solar **eclipses.** Like the Babylonians, the Chinese tried to predict the motion of the planets. Around the same time, Greek astronomer Aristarchus of Samos proposed that Earth revolves around the sun. This was a revolutionary claim, as scientists before this time strongly believed that the sun and other bodies orbited, or circled around, Earth. **Astronomers** disagreed about the position of Earth and other stars in space for many years.

Greek astronomer Aristarchus of Samos (310? B.C.-230? B.C.) claimed that Earth revolves around the sun. He was the first person known to make this claim. Aristarchus also used geometry to try to calculate the sizes of the sun and moon and their distances from Earth. Although his method was correct, his calculations were wrong.

c. 200 B.C.

c. 100 B.C.

Early Greek astronomer Hipparchus (180 B.C.?-125 B.C.?) may have drawn the first catalog of stars. This log recorded each star's brightness and position in the sky. Hipparchus also discovered a slow eastward motion of the stars.

Astronomer Ptolemy (A.D. 100?-A.D. 165?) wrote his observations in a 13-part work known as the *Almagest*. In this document, Ptolemy claimed that everything in the universe moves either toward or around Earth's center. He also cataloged stars and developed a way of using mathematics to record star positions. People accepted Ptolemy's system until the mid-1500's.

c. A.D. 150

During the A.D. 100's, early astronomer Ptolemy attempted to explain the **retrograde motion** of the planets while living in Alexandria, Egypt. He said the planets moved in small circles called **epicycles.** The epicycles, in turn, moved along a larger circle called a **deferent.** Like Aristotle, Ptolemy believed that the planets revolved around Earth. But Ptolemy claimed that Earth was not quite at the center of the deferents. This, he thought, was why the planets and the sun appeared to speed up and slow down during the year.

Beginning in the 800's, scholars living in the Middle East developed and improved upon Ptolemy's theories. They did not challenge the central idea that the heavenly bodies orbited a motionless Earth. Before the invention of telescopes in the early 1600's, people relied on eyesight alone to gather information about the stars.

Mayan astronomers observed the positions of the sun, moon, planets, and stars. The Maya lived in what is now Mexico and Central America. They built stone observatories, or buildings, from which to study the sky. They created tables that predicted eclipses and described the motions of the planet Venus. The Maya also made an accurate calendar of 365 days based upon the orbit of Earth around the sun.

c. A.D. 300

c. A.D. 850

Ancient Chinese peoples experimented with small **rockets** in fireworks and warfare.

Chapter 2

The Copernican Revolution
1300's—1780's

The Renaissance (a word meaning *rebirth*) was a period of European history from about the 1300's to the 1600's when the study of sciences, art, literature, and history gained new significance to people. In the mid-1400's, Johannes Gutenberg (1395?-1468?) from Germany invented the printing press. This invention allowed copies of books to be printed quickly by machines instead of copied slowly by hand. Printed books—including those on astronomy—helped spread new ideas about the universe rapidly throughout Europe.

1543

Nicolaus Copernicus (1473-1543) produced his great work, *On the Revolutions of the Heavenly Spheres*. In this book, he stated that Earth and other planets revolve around the sun. He showed how Earth's motion could be used to explain irregularities in the movements of other bodies in space. Copernicus argued that planets do not actually change course: a planet's apparent

retrograde motion is caused by its position relative to Earth as they orbit the sun at different speeds. His groundbreaking ideas, now known as *Copernican theory*, eventually changed the way people thought about the **solar system.**

1572

Danish astronomer Tycho Brahe (1546-1601) built astronomy instruments to precisely measure planetary movements. In 1572, Brahe saw a **supernova.** This sighting helped disprove the ancient idea that no change could happen in the universe beyond the orbit of Earth's moon.

The next great advance in understanding the universe came from Polish astronomer Nicolaus Copernicus. He developed a theory that Earth is a moving planet. He also argued that Earth and the other planets revolve around the sun. Though most **astronomers** at the time disagreed with him, Copernicus's ideas were essentially correct. He is considered the founder of modern astronomy.

Meanwhile, Italian astronomer Galileo Galilei used a new device to study the planets—the telescope. With a simple telescope, his startling discoveries convinced him that Copernicus was correct in his theory that the planets revolve around the sun. Both Copernicus and Galileo's theories caused arguments among people who believed in one idea or the other. However, the two scientists' theories made lasting impressions on the field of astronomy.

German mathematician and astronomer Johannes Kepler (1571-1630) discovered three laws of planetary motion. His findings showed that planets move around the sun in elliptical, or oval, paths, proving Copernican theory.

1609–1619

1608

Dutch eyeglass maker Hans Lippershey (1570?-1619) is believed to have invented the first telescope.

1609

Italian astronomer Galileo Galilei (1564-1642) built his first telescope in 1609. The simplest form of a refracting *telescope* consists of a special glass lens at each end of a long tube. The lenses magnify, or enlarge, distant objects. Looking through the telescope, Galileo discovered that the moon is not perfectly smooth, as Aristotle and Ptolemy thought. He saw mountains and craters on the moon's surface. In 1610, he discovered four moons circling Jupiter. Galileo revealed his discoveries in a paper titled *The Sidereal Messenger*. This proved that an object other than Earth could be at the center of revolving bodies. His later observation that Venus had phases, or stages, like the moon, proved that Venus circled the sun, not Earth.

The Copernican Revolution
1300's—1780's

From the 1600's through the 1700's, **astronomers** made many new observations and discoveries about the universe. In the early 1600's, Galileo explained how Earth could be in motion—even though people feel like they are standing perfectly still on its surface. He developed mathematical laws to explain his findings. These discoveries helped lead to his great work called the *Dialogue Concerning the Two Chief World Systems*. Published in 1632, this book compared the theory of Aristotle and Ptolemy with that of Copernicus. In his presentation, Galileo clearly favored the Copernican view. But his arguments brought him into conflict with the Roman Catholic Church.

Galileo published the *Dialogue Concerning the Two Chief World Systems*, supporting Copernican theory.

1632

English astronomer Edmond Halley (1656-1742) observed the comet that would become known as *Halley's Comet*. This comet appears in the sky about every 76 years. Later, Halley also showed that stars have proper motion—that is, they change position in relation to one another.

1682

Galileo's findings contributed to a larger societal movement called the *Enlightenment.* Enlightenment philosophers believed truth could be discovered only with reason and science. They thought that the advancement of knowledge—including scientific knowledge of the universe—was the best way to improve humanity. Scholars published such knowledge in printed books.

In 1682, English astronomer Edmond Halley observed a **comet.** He suggested it was the same comet that was sighted in 1531 and 1607. Halley correctly predicted the comet's return in 1758, but did not live to see it pass by Earth again. In 1781, British astronomer Sir William Herschel discovered the planet Uranus. It was the first planet discovered using a telescope. At this time, scientists knew of seven planets in our **galaxy**—Mercury, Venus, Earth, Mars, Jupiter, Saturn, and Uranus.

British astronomer Sir William Herschel (1738-1822) discovered the planet Uranus. It was the first new planet discovered in hundreds of years.

1781

English astronomer and mathematician Sir Isaac Newton (1642-1727) published his Laws of Motion in a paper titled *Principia mathematica.* Newton's most important discovery was a universal force called *gravitation.* Newton realized that the same force, called *gravity,* makes a pebble fall to the ground and keeps the moon traveling around Earth. He found that simple mathematical equations could explain both falling pebbles and moving planets. Newton's discovery proved beyond all doubt that the Copernican theory was correct.

1687

c. 1750

Between 1750 and 1784, French astronomer Charles Messier (1730-1817) made a list of the most prominent *nebulae* (clouds of dust particles and gas that appear fuzzy and unclear in regions of the night sky).

Chapter 3

A Timeline of Space Exploration

Modern Astronomy
Late 1700's—1940's

During the late 1700's and 1800's, a rapid development in society known as the Industrial Revolution caused great changes in society and technology. People started using steam-powered machines to produce many goods quickly and inexpensively, including glass and metals used to build telescopes.

In this time of change, **astronomers** continued their studies. Astronomy clubs and societies were established. People at observatories, or places at which to

Italian astronomer Giuseppe Piazzi (1746-1826) discovered a small planetlike object found between the orbits of Mars and Jupiter. He named the body Ceres (below).

The following year, German astronomer Wilhelm Olbers (1758-1840) discovered another small body in the **Main Belt.** He called it Pallas. Sir William Herschel named these and other orbiting bodies asteroids. Today, Ceres is considered both an asteroid and a **dwarf planet.** It is the largest of all asteroids.

EARL ROSSE'S GREAT TELESCOPE

1801

1845

Irish astronomer William Parsons (1800-1867), Earl of Rosse, built a large reflecting telescope that used mirrors instead of lenses to collect and focus light. His telescope had a mirror 6 feet (1.8 meters) across the base. This improvement allowed him to see that many *nebulae* (clouds of dust and gas) are spiral in shape.

study the sky, around the globe worked together to create a map of the heavens. Scientists started to understand what materials make up the sun and stars. From 1859 to 1862, German scientists Robert Bunsen and Gustav Kirchhoff used light patterns to discover the chemicals that form the sun. Bunsen and Kirchhoff's discovery began a new branch of astronomy called *spectroscopy*. Spectroscopy is the study of light broken up into its individual colors. It is used to study the makeup of stars.

In the late 1700's, astronomers discovered the **Main Belt.** Astronomers found numerous **asteroids** within the Main Belt region. The smallest asteroids can be pebble-sized and the largest can be miles wide. The first asteroid to be discovered was Ceres (*SIHR eez*) in 1801.

German astronomer Johann Galle (1812-1910) saw Neptune in the sky using a telescope. He based his search on the work of astronomers John C. Adams (1819-1892) of the United Kingdom and Urbain J. J. Le Verrier (1811-1877) of France. Working independently, Adams and Le Verrier both calculated and predicted where in the sky Neptune could be found.

1846

1859-1862

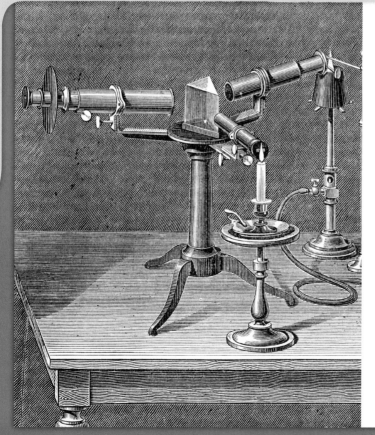

German scientists Robert Bunsen (1811-1899) and Gustav Kirchhoff (1824-1887) studied the sun's glowing **atmosphere.** They experimented with different chemical elements that make up a planet's environment. They found that light emitted from an element produces a particular spectrum. (A spectrum is a band of colors formed when a beam of light is passed through a triangular piece of glass called a *prism.*) Bunsen and Kirchoff studied the light given off by the sun to determine the chemical elements present in the star.

Modern Astronomy
Late 1700's—1940's

The Industrial Revolution brought new technologies that helped people invent flying machines, including the first airplane. But airplanes could not be used to travel into space. The invention of the **rocket** made space travel possible. In the early 1900's, Konstantin Tsiolkovsky of Russia, Robert Goddard of the United States, and Hermann Oberth (1894-1989) of Germany worked independently to address many of the technical problems of *rocketry* (rocket science). English **astronomer** and mathematician Sir Isaac Newton's laws of motion heavily influenced scientists' thoughts on the development of rockets.

Russian high school teacher Konstantin Tsiolkovsky (1857-1935) wrote *The Exploration of Cosmic Space by Means of Reaction Devices.* This was the first scientific paper about the use of rockets for space travel.

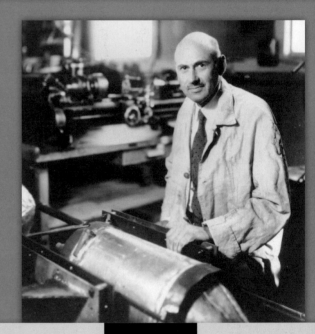

1903

1915

1919

German-born physicist Albert Einstein (1879-1955) announced his *theory of general relativity.* Combined with his *theory of special relativity*, which he developed in 1905, Einstein's ideas transformed astronomers' view of the universe. Space and time were shown to be woven together in a fabric of sorts that massive objects could distort or even tear. Measurements of all kinds, including time, can vary from one observer to the next. Matter can turn into energy, and energy can turn into matter.

United States scientist Robert Goddard's (1882-1945) paper, *A Method of Reaching Extreme Altitudes,* explained how rockets could be used to explore the upper **atmosphere.** His claim that a rocket could reach the moon was mocked in the newspapers. In 1926, Goddard's team built the world's first liquid-fueled rocket.

These scientists' work led to the use of rockets in World War II (1939–1945). During the war, Germany used specialized rockets called *missiles* as long-range, destructive weapons. After World War II, the U.S. and the Soviet Union emerged as the most powerful countries—called the two *superpowers*. The two countries competed for influence in the world's politics. They both recruited German rocket engineers to help develop military missiles and rockets for space exploration. This intense rivalry became known as the Cold War, which lasted over 40 years.

In 1949, the United States launched the world's first two-stage rocket to reach space. Each stage, or section, of the rocket has an engine and fuel. When the fuel in one stage is used up, that stage drops off the rocket and falls back down to Earth.

1924

American astronomer Edwin Hubble (1889-1953) studied the spiral-shaped Andromeda Nebula. He found that it was actually a distant **galaxy,** separate from the Milky Way. The Milky Way contains the sun, Earth, and other objects in our **solar system.** Before this discovery, many scientists believed that all celestial objects were part of the Milky Way. In 1929, Hubble discovered that the farther apart galaxies are from each other, the faster they move away from each other. He concluded that the universe is expanding at a uniform, or constant, rate.

1930

American astronomer Clyde Tombaugh (1906-1997) discovered Pluto. This body was called a planet until scientists reclassified it as a **dwarf planet** in 2006.

Chapter 4

First Steps into Space
1950's—1972

The Cold War rivalry between the United States and Soviet Union space programs became known as the *space race.* On October 4, 1957, the Soviet Union launched the world's first **artificial satellite,** named Sputnik, to orbit Earth. This great achievement encouraged scientists in the U.S. space program to improve their work. The U.S. launched the Explorer I satellite in 1958. A month after Sputnik, the Soviets launched another artificial satellite, Sputnik 2. It carried a dog named Laika. Scientists hoped to learn about the effects of space travel on a living being.

1958

July 29: A United States governmental space agency called the National Aeronautics and Space Administration (NASA) was established. NASA plans and carries out all U.S. space missions.

1961

April 12: Soviet pilot and **cosmonaut** Yuri Gagarin (1934-1968) was the first person in space. He orbited Earth one time. The mission took 108 minutes.

In 1959, the Soviet **probe** Luna 1 was the first probe to travel close to the moon, passing within several thousand miles of the moon's surface. Luna 1 sent back scientific measurements to Earth. It was the first data scientists received from a moon probe. Both nations launched probes towards Mars and Venus in the 1960's.

By the early 1960's, the United States and the Soviet Union developed spacecraft powered by **rockets** that could carry humans. The first person in space was Soviet air force pilot Yuri Gagarin. About a month later, American Alan Shepard rocketed into the **atmosphere.** In 1962, John Glenn (1921-) became the first American to orbit Earth. He orbited Earth three times in less than five hours. The Soviets launched the first multiperson space capsule in 1964. It carried three cosmonauts who spent 24 hours orbiting Earth.

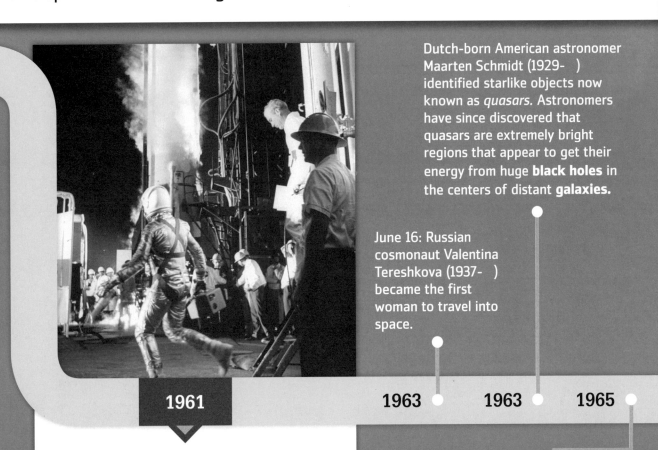

Dutch-born American astronomer Maarten Schmidt (1929-) identified starlike objects now known as *quasars.* Astronomers have since discovered that quasars are extremely bright regions that appear to get their energy from huge **black holes** in the centers of distant **galaxies.**

June 16: Russian cosmonaut Valentina Tereshkova (1937-) became the first woman to travel into space.

1961

1963

1963

1965

May 5: The United States sends the first American, Alan Shepard (1923-1998), into space. On May 25, U.S. President John F. Kennedy made a historic speech to Congress. In his speech, Kennedy boldly predicted that the U.S. would send astronauts to the moon by the end of the 1960's.

March 18: Soviet cosmonaut Alexei A. Leonov (1934-) became the first human to step outside a spacecraft and float freely in space.

First Steps into Space
1950's—1972

During the mid-1960's, space programs expanded at a rapid pace. More astronauts traveled into space for longer periods of time. Both the United States and the Soviet Union aimed to be the first country to send a human to the moon. In 1969, U.S. astronauts "won" the space race by being the first nation to land a person on the moon.

To prepare for the moon landing, NASA conducted several Apollo missions. The Apollo spacecraft was a new design made of three parts. Each part of the spacecraft played a role in landing on the moon. While training inside the

1969

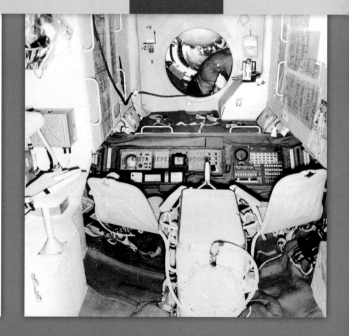

1971

April 19: The Soviet Union launched the first *space station*, Salyut 1. A space station is an orbiting **artificial satellite** that has enough room for several astronauts to live and work for long periods of time. Three **cosmonauts** spent 24 days aboard Salyut 1, where they made medical observations and performed experiments.

July 20: U.S. astronaut Neil Armstrong (1930-2012) was the first person to walk on the moon. Before leaving his space capsule, Armstrong turned on a live television camera. The world watched as he walked down a ladder and planted his left foot on the solid surface. He famously said, "That's one small step for a man, one giant leap for mankind." Buzz Aldrin (1930-) soon joined him on the moonwalk (above). Michael Collins (1930-) stayed aboard the spacecraft. After 21 hours on the moon, Apollo 11 headed back to Earth.

spacecraft for Apollo 1 in 1967, the spacecraft caught fire, and all three U.S. astronauts were killed on the launchpad at Cape Canaveral, Florida. This marked the first great tragedy of the United States space program. After this accident, NASA scientists improved the Apollo spacecraft, changing its wiring and exit door. When several more Apollo missions proved successful, NASA was ready to attempt a moon landing. Apollo 11 launched in July 1969 carrying three U.S. astronauts: Neil Armstrong, Buzz Aldrin, and Michael Collins. The eight-day mission was a success. Armstrong was the first person to walk on the moon.

More Apollo moon landings followed. Astronauts took soil and rocks from the moon's surface back to Earth to study. Astronauts from Apollo 15 used a lunar **rover** to explore more of the moon than ever before.

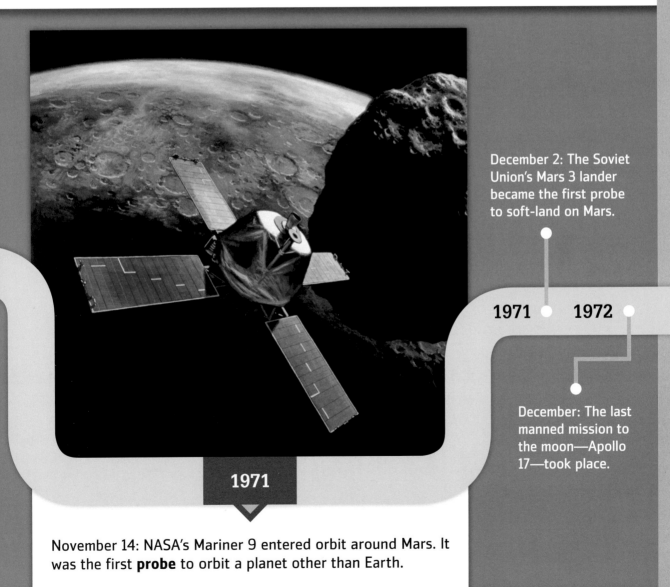

December 2: The Soviet Union's Mars 3 lander became the first probe to soft-land on Mars.

1971   1972

December: The last manned mission to the moon—Apollo 17—took place.

1971

November 14: NASA's Mariner 9 entered orbit around Mars. It was the first **probe** to orbit a planet other than Earth.

Chapter 5

Exploring the Planets
1973—1986

After accomplishing several moon landings, space programs turned their attention toward exploring other planets. NASA sent the **probe** Pioneer 11 on a mission to Jupiter in 1973. After that, the probe was redirected to Saturn, arriving there in 1979. In 1974 and 1976, the United States launched two German-built Helios probes to measure solar **radiation** within Mercury's orbit. In 1976, U.S. probes Viking 1 and Viking 2 landed on Mars. Probes were also sent to Venus, where they created rough maps of the planet's surface.

November 3: United States Mariner 10 was launched. It flew past Venus in February 1974. Then it made three passes near Mercury in 1974 and 1975. It was the first spacecraft to reach Mercury.

1975

1973

1973

July: The Apollo-Soyuz Test Project was the first joint mission of U.S. astronauts and Soviet **cosmonauts.** The U.S. Apollo capsule successfully linked up in space with the Soviet Soyuz capsule. This project was the first international docking in space.

May 14: Skylab was released into orbit. It was the first U.S. space station and it was damaged during the launch. The crew worked outside the station to make repairs during their 28-day mission. The next crews aboard Skylab performed many types of scientific experiments in space, including growing plants. Skylab also had a special room with six telescopes for studying the sun.

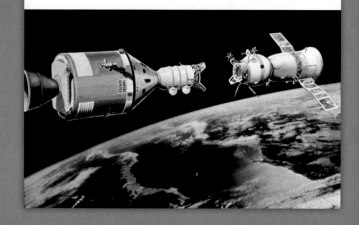

During the 1970's, the Soviet Union continued to launch Salyut space stations. Salyut 6 (1977) had two docking ports, allowing a second crew or a resupply vehicle to visit the station. The ability for other spaceships to come and go from the orbiting station greatly extended the space station's working life. Salyut 6 operated for almost five years. Later, in the 1980's, the Soviets launched the much larger Mir space station.

Space suits were also improved during this time. Special suits help to protect astronauts from the extreme heat and cold in space. Modern space suits are made from many layers of flexible, airtight materials. Tight mechanical seals connect the pieces of the space suit, including the gloves, helmet, and breathing equipment.

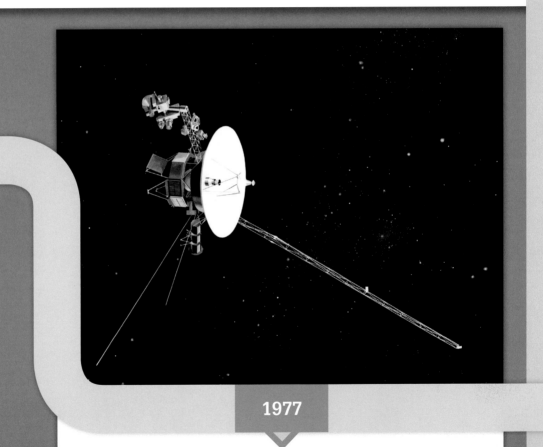

1976

July 20: The U.S. probe Viking 1 landed on Mars. Viking 2 touched down on September 3. They operated for several years taking photographs, measuring surface weather, and conducting experiments to try and detect life.

1977

NASA launched the probes Voyager 1 and Voyager 2 to explore the outer **solar system.** From 1979 through 1989, the Voyager probes visited Jupiter, Saturn, Uranus, and Neptune. Today, both Voyagers are farther away from Earth than the distant **dwarf planet** Pluto. Both probes continue to send scientific information to NASA.

Exploring the Planets
1973—1986

The space race between the United States and Soviet Union came to an end in the late 1970's, as both countries focused on their own missions. In 1981, the U.S. began its **space shuttle** program. This new type of spacecraft could be reused to *shuttle* (move back and forth) items between Earth and space. The space shuttles were designed to blast off like a **rocket** and land on a runway like an airplane. The large shuttles carried **artificial satellites,** space **probes,** and fresh supplies to space stations. They retrieved mission crews, scientific experiments, and old satellites to bring back to Earth. Such shuttles could carry up to eight people.

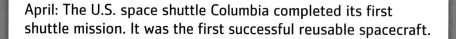

April: The U.S. space shuttle Columbia completed its first shuttle mission. It was the first successful reusable spacecraft.

1981

Two Soviet probes, Venera 15 and 16, used radar equipment to map most of Venus's northern hemisphere.

1983 **1984**

United States President Ronald Reagan (1911-2004) approved the building of a large, permanent space station. This structure would eventually become the International Space Station (ISS).

U.S. space shuttle missions continued until 2011. Though the U.S. program was successful in many ways, a tragic accident happened in 1986. The space shuttle Challenger broke apart in midair just after liftoff, killing all members on board. This tragedy caused NASA to reevaluate its shuttle design and temporarily stop the shuttle program.

During the 1980's, people made the first contact with **comets.** The U.S. probe International Cometary Explorer was the first to reach a comet, in 1985. Later that year, Giotto, launched by the European Space Agency (ESA), passed within 375 miles (600 kilometers) of Halley's Comet. Giotto sent back dramatic images in 1986. Two Soviet probes passed close to Halley's Comet the following year.

March 14: The European Space Agency's first deep-space mission, Giotto, passed by Halley's Comet.

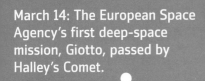

1986   1986

January 28: U.S. space shuttle Challenger was destroyed only 73 seconds into its flight. This accident killed all seven astronauts on board. When NASA investigated the disaster, they found that rings made to seal rocket fuel had leaked when the launch went forward on too cold a day. NASA began making rings out of a different material.

1986

February 20: Soviet space station Mir was launched into orbit. Mir had two docking ports and four other hatches, or entryways. The station was designed like the spokes of a wheel. Mir had a hub in the center, with modules that attached and extended outward from the hub.

Chapter 6

New Discoveries
1987—1990's

The U.S. resumed their **space shuttle** missions in 1988. In the late 1980's, the U.S. launched several other missions, including the space **probes** Galileo (1989), sent to explore Jupiter, its moons, and rings; Magellan (1989), on a mission to map Venus; and Ulysses (1990), sent to study the sun. Magellan reached its destination in 1990, mapping almost the entire surface of Venus. These images revealed a varied landscape on the surface of Venus. Ulysses made observations of the sun during 1994-1995, 2000-2001, and 2007-2008.

New records were set for human spaceflight. Between 1987 and 1988, two Soviet **cosmonauts** spent 366 consecutive days in orbit aboard the space station Mir. This helped prove that people could survive in space for long periods of time.

1987

1987-1988

February 23: **Supernova** 1987A could be seen with the naked eye from Earth's southern hemisphere, or half. It was the closest observed supernova since 1604. This sighting gave modern astronomers their first chance to study a nearby exploding star.

The United States Cosmic Background Explorer (COBE) satellite was launched in 1989. It investigated the cosmic microwave background (CMB) **radiation** of the universe. CMB radiation is energy left over from the early history of the universe. This energy formed as the early universe expanded. American physicists Arno Penzias (1933-) and Robert W. Wilson (1936-) discovered CMB radiation in the 1960's. Penzias and Wilson each received half of the 1978 Nobel Prize in physics for the discovery.

Meanwhile, the Voyager spacecrafts continued their journeys through the outer **solar system.** Voyager 2 flew past Neptune in August 1989. It sent back stunning images of geyserlike eruptions on Triton, a moon of Neptune.

1990

1992

April 24: The space shuttle Discovery launched the Hubble Space Telescope into Earth's orbit. It was named after influential American astronomer Edwin Hubble. The Hubble is a reflecting telescope with a giant light-gathering mirror 94 inches (240 centimeters) in diameter. Astronomers control the telescope from Earth. They use the powerful telescope to study never-before-seen regions of space. The Hubble Telescope can provide sharper images of celestial objects than Earth-based telescopes because it views space without looking through Earth's **atmosphere.** NASA expects the telescope to function until at least 2020.

Polish-born American astronomer Aleksander Wolszczan (1946-) and American Dale Frail (1961-) discovered two **exoplanets** and a possible third in orbit around a **pulsar** in the constellation, or star formation, Virgo. The rapidly spinning star gives off radiation that arrives on Earth in regular patterns.

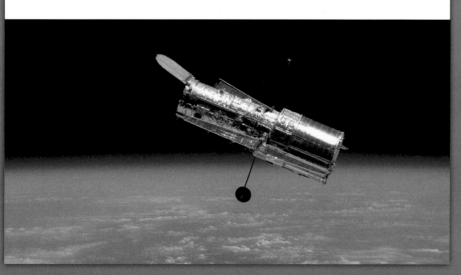

New Discoveries
1987—1990's

In 1991, the Soviet Union broke apart into separate countries. Russia had been the most important republic in the Soviet Union. After the breakup, Russia set up new political, legal, and economic systems, but it kept the former Soviet Union space program in place. Russian scientists and **cosmonauts** continued their work exploring the universe.

In 1992, **astronomers** found the first planets circling a star other than our sun. These orbiting planets are known as **exoplanets.** The star is called a **pulsar.** In 1995, astronomers found the first exoplanet orbiting a sunlike star, 51 Pegasi, in

December: Crew members from the shuttle Endeavour repaired the orbiting Hubble Space Telescope after NASA discovered an error in its main mirror.

1993

1994

January 25: U.S. lunar probe Clementine launched. During its four-month mission, Clementine took more than 2 million photos of the moon. The probe also discovered signs of ice in craters around the moon's south poles. More moon probes were sent in the late 1990's.

1992

English-born American astronomer David Jewitt (1958-) and Vietnamese-born American astronomer Jane Luu (1963-) discovered the first **Kuiper belt** object (**KBO**). Astronomers estimate there are thousands of KBO's made of rock and ice.

the constellation Pegasus. That same year, *cosmologists* (scientists who study the origin and development of the universe) made another huge discovery. They announced that the COBE satellite had discovered small variations in the temperature of the CMB **radiation.** The radiation energy differed from one part of the sky to another. Scientists believe the variations show that matter began to clump together during the early formation of the universe. Over billions of years, they believe these clumps grew into the **galaxies.**

After a gap of 22 years, NASA returned to the moon. The unpiloted **probe** Clementine went into lunar orbit in January 1994. From February to May, Clementine studied the moon's surface while in orbit.

1995

March 22: Soviet cosmonaut Valery Polyakov (1942-   ) returned to Earth from Mir after he spent a record 438 consecutive days in space. In 2016, NASA astronaut Scott Kelly (1964-   ) spent 340 days in space, the most for an American astronaut.

1995

1995

June 29: 20 years after the Apollo-Soyuz Test Project, U.S. **space shuttle** Atlantis docked with Russia's Mir space station.

December: NASA's Galileo probe reached Jupiter and dropped another probe into Jupiter's **atmosphere.**

New Discoveries
1987—1990's

In the mid 1990's, NASA sent several **probes** to continue exploring the **solar system.** After a 20-year absence, probes returned to Mars to map its surface. A Mars **rover** named Sojourner was carried to the planet to explore the rocks and soil at ground level. Numerous probes blasted off to study **asteroids** at close range.

In 1998, cosmologists made the startling discovery that the expansion of the universe is speeding up. Studies of distant **supernovae** showed that they were farther away from Earth than predicted. Scientists concluded that an unknown force was countering the effects of gravity. This force causes the expansion of the

September 7: U.S. astronaut Shannon Lucid (1943-   ) broke the world record for consecutive days in space by a woman. She spent a total of 188 days in space, mostly aboard the Russian space station Mir. Lucid returned from space on September 26, 1996.

1996

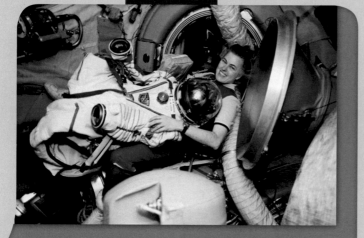

1996

June 27: NASA's Near Earth Asteroid Rendezvous (NEAR) probe flew within several hundred miles of the asteroid Mathilde in 1997. It went into orbit around another asteroid, Eros, in 2000. (The probe was renamed NEAR-Shoemaker in honor of planetary scientist Gene Shoemaker [1928-1997]).

1997

November 7: NASA sent the Mars Global Surveyor probe to map the planet's surface while in orbit. The probe used such advanced tools as a laser and a high-resolution camera to calculate the height and depth of the planet's physical features. The tools also identified some of the minerals on Mars's surface.

universe to increase in speed. Scientists called this mysterious force *dark energy*.

Also in 1998, the first part of the International Space Station (ISS) was placed into orbit. The ISS is a joint satellite project involving NASA and 15 space agencies, including those of Russia, Japan, Europe, and Canada. It serves as an important research laboratory where crew members from around the world can conduct experiments in microgravity. (Microgravity is a condition of having so little gravity that objects are almost weightless.) ISS experiments have included growing crops, testing spiders, and studying human blood. The ISS is also designed to create conditions similar to those on Earth. Astronauts can breathe, eat, drink, sleep, exercise, bathe, and receive medical treatment while aboard the ISS.

July: NASA used the Pathfinder probe to test a new landing system on the surface of Mars. It released a six-wheeled rover vehicle called Sojourner to explore the surface. Sojourner could move around by itself and avoid obstacles. It carried a scientific device that analyzed the rocks and soil. Both Pathfinder and Sojourner sent remarkable data back to Earth.

1997

1998

Astronauts from many nations began to assemble the ISS as the space station orbited Earth.

Chapter 7

Space Exploration Today
Early 2000's—Today

The early 2000's witnessed an increase in space exploration, as such countries as China joined the spacefaring nations. Various spacecraft were sent from Earth to many parts of the **solar system,** including Earth's moon, Mars, Mercury, and Saturn. NASA's Stardust **probe** gathered samples from the *coma* (outer cloudy part) of **Comet** Wild 2. NASA's NEAR-Shoemaker spacecraft landed on the **asteroid** Eros. The European Space Agency (ESA) launched its first mission to orbit the moon, the SMART-1 satellite.

2003

August: Mars passed closer to Earth than it had in about 60,000 years. As Mars came near, scientists launched three probes from Earth to study the planet. The ESA's Mars Express probe went into orbit around Mars. In January 2004, Spirit and Opportunity, two United States rovers, landed on Mars. They carried instruments to study the planet's soil and rocks. In late 2004, after studying data collected by all three spacecraft, scientists suggested that Mars once had large amounts of liquid water. They later found that the planet's south pole contains so much water-ice that it would cover the planet in water 36 feet (11 meters) deep if it melted.

2001

Russia guides the Mir out of its orbit after about 15 years of use. Eventually, a space station is in an orbit position so low that it hits Earth's atmosphere and is burned up. Mir had become too costly for Russia to keep operating.

Scientists were especially interested in studying Mars. The most stunning find on the planet was the discovery of water-ice. In 2002, NASA's Mars Odyssey probe found large amounts of ice within 3 feet (1 meter) of the planet's surface. In 2003, the ESA's Mars Express probe detected ice near the planet's south pole. Mars Express also found a gas called *methane* in the Martian **atmosphere.** This gas is a possible indicator of life on Mars.

Tragedy struck NASA's space program on February 1, 2003. The **space shuttle** Columbia broke apart as it reentered Earth's atmosphere. The disaster took the lives of all seven crew members. NASA halted all upcoming shuttle flights. In August, investigators reported that the accident was caused by damage to a wing during liftoff. This caused the shuttle to break apart as it tried to land.

2003

2004

October: China became the third nation to launch a human into space. Astronaut Yang Liwei (1965-) orbited Earth for 21 hours.

July 1: The Cassini probe went into orbit around Saturn. It was the first spacecraft to reach the planet. Cassini carried another smaller probe named Huygens. In 2005, it dropped Huygens into the atmosphere of Titan, Saturn's largest moon. Together, Cassini and Huygens study Saturn, its rings, and its moons. NASA and European space agencies work together on this ongoing mission.

Space Exploration Today
Early 2000's—Today

In 2005, the discovery of Eris and two other large **KBO's,** Haumea and Makemake, caused debate among astronomers over the definition of the term *planet*. In August 2006, the International Astronomical Union (IAU) announced the creation of a new category of celestial bodies called **dwarf planets.** Dwarf planets would include Eris, Pluto, Haumea, Makemake, and Ceres, the largest body in the **asteroid** belt. Until this time, Pluto was considered a planet. But it was reclassified as a dwarf planet because it is not much bigger than Eris. On January 19, 2006, NASA launched the New Horizons **probe** on the first mission to explore Pluto.

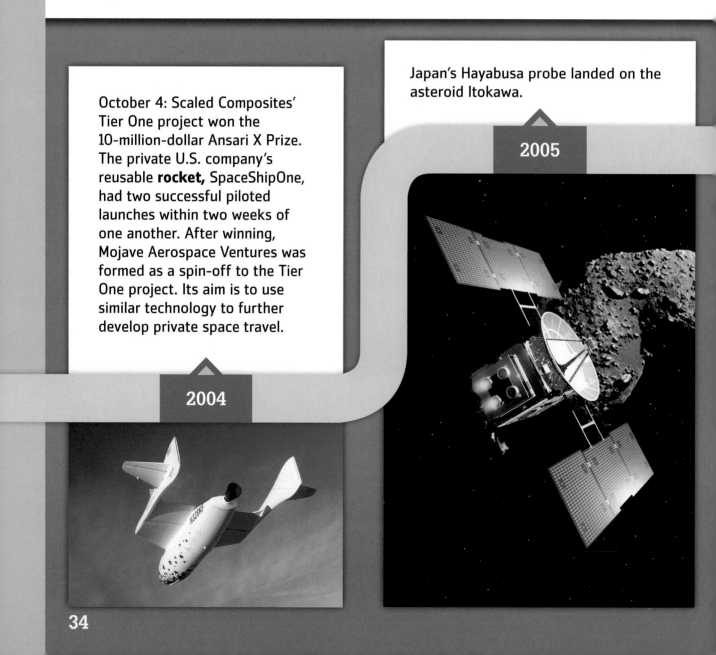

October 4: Scaled Composites' Tier One project won the 10-million-dollar Ansari X Prize. The private U.S. company's reusable **rocket,** SpaceShipOne, had two successful piloted launches within two weeks of one another. After winning, Mojave Aerospace Ventures was formed as a spin-off to the Tier One project. Its aim is to use similar technology to further develop private space travel.

Japan's Hayabusa probe landed on the asteroid Itokawa.

2005

2004

Between 2007 and 2009, the United States, Japan, China, and India all launched spacecraft in orbit around the moon. Every mission used scientific instruments to map the lunar surface. India's Chandrayaan-1 satellite released a probe that landed on the surface, making India the fourth country to reach the moon. The U.S. Lunar Crater Observation and Sensing Satellite (LCROSS) detected the presence of water-ice near the moon's south pole in 2009.

Many private companies developed services to compete with the national and international space organizations. A U.S. organization, the X Prize Foundation, funded the X Prize (later the Ansari X Prize) competition to encourage private space travel. The group offered millions of dollars to privately funded teams interested in building and launching spacecraft capable of carrying passengers.

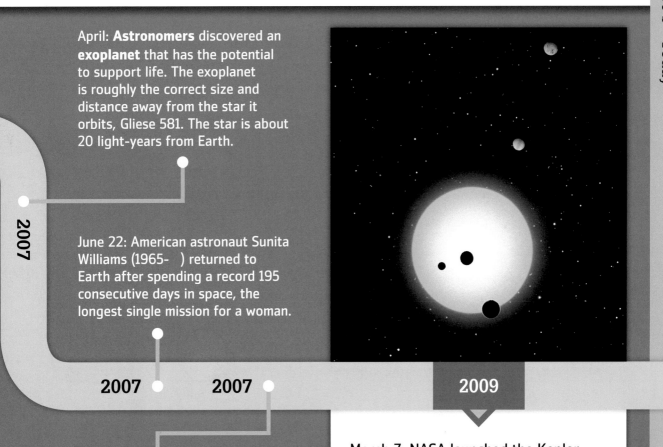

2007

April: **Astronomers** discovered an **exoplanet** that has the potential to support life. The exoplanet is roughly the correct size and distance away from the star it orbits, Gliese 581. The star is about 20 light-years from Earth.

June 22: American astronaut Sunita Williams (1965-   ) returned to Earth after spending a record 195 consecutive days in space, the longest single mission for a woman.

2007   **2007**   **2009**

September: The X Prize Foundation announced a prize for a privately funded mission to Earth's moon. The winner would be awarded up to 25 million dollars for landing a robot on the lunar surface, traveling a certain distance, and sending images and data back to Earth. If completed, the online-search company Google, Inc. planned to pay the winner's award.

March 7: NASA launched the Kepler space probe. This probe has a powerful telescope that is designed to look for distant small, rocky planets that may support life. It is named after influential German astronomer and mathematician Johannes Kepler.

Space Exploration Today
Early 2000's—Today

During the 2010's, researchers continued developing new technologies that could cut the costs of spaceflight. The **space shuttle** flew its final mission in 2011. Scientists and engineers hoped to replace it with a reusable craft that could take off and land either horizontally like an airplane or vertically like a **rocket,** and control its own rockets to go into orbit.

Space agencies and private companies are deciding on the next stage of space exploration. Some experts believe that humans will visit Mars within the next few decades. Other scientists have suggested that both the moon and Mars could

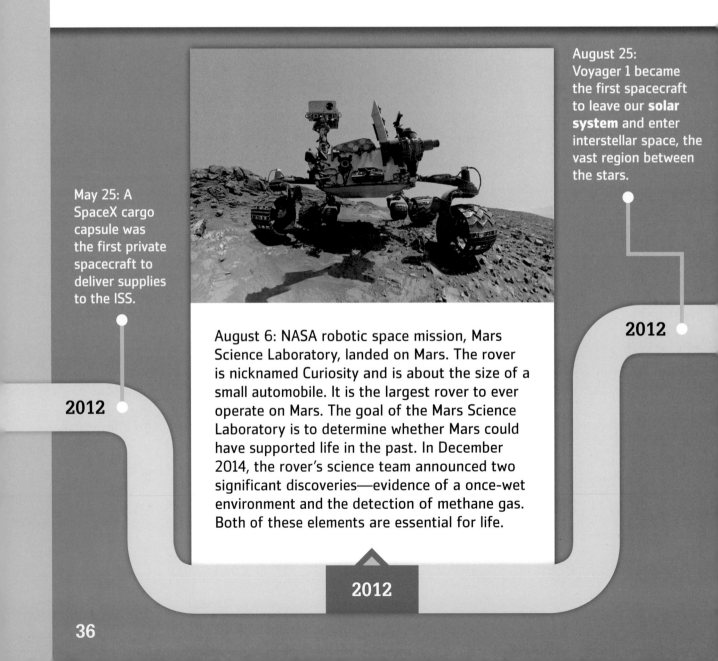

August 25: Voyager 1 became the first spacecraft to leave our **solar system** and enter interstellar space, the vast region between the stars.

May 25: A SpaceX cargo capsule was the first private spacecraft to deliver supplies to the ISS.

August 6: NASA robotic space mission, Mars Science Laboratory, landed on Mars. The rover is nicknamed Curiosity and is about the size of a small automobile. It is the largest rover to ever operate on Mars. The goal of the Mars Science Laboratory is to determine whether Mars could have supported life in the past. In December 2014, the rover's science team announced two significant discoveries—evidence of a once-wet environment and the detection of methane gas. Both of these elements are essential for life.

2012

2012

2012

support long-term bases where humans can live and research. But before these bases are established, many technical advances must be made. Doctors must research the risks to human health from traveling such large distances away from Earth. Astronauts would need special equipment to shield them from dangerous **radiation.** Supplies, food, and fuel would have to be readily sent to the Martian bases. Scientists continue to work together to make a mission to Mars possible.

Throughout time, scientists have learned much about the stars and sky. In the future, **astronomers** and such other scientists as astrophysicists will explore more of the unknown parts of the universe. The lasting spirit of curiosity will help future astronomers and other scientists meet their space exploration goals.

November: Astronomers announced evidence of a *rogue planet*. This is the first planet found traveling through space without orbiting a star.

Scientists from the Laser Interferometer Gravitational-Wave Observatory (LIGO) announced that they had detected gravitational waves. Violent interactions of large celestial bodies create these ripples in the fabric of space-time. In 1915, Albert Einstein had predicted their existence, but it took about 100 years for scientists to detect the waves.

2016

2012   **2015**

July 14: NASA's New Horizons probe flew about 7,800 miles (12,500 kilometers) above the surface of Pluto. It was the first spacecraft to explore and take photos of the **dwarf planet.**

Glossary

artificial satellite   a human-made object placed in orbit around Earth or some other body in space.

asteroid   a small, rocky or metallic body that orbits a star.

astronomer   a scientist who studies the universe and the objects in it.

atmosphere   the blanket of air surrounding Earth.

black hole   an invisible region of space that has such an intense gravitational pull that nothing, not even light, can escape from it.

comet   a celestial object made up of a *nucleus* (core) of ice and dust. When near the sun, it produces a tail of gas and dust particles pointing away from the sun.

cosmonaut   an astronaut, especially a Russian astronaut.

deferent   according to ancient astronomers, the large circular shape along which epicycles moved.

dwarf planet   a small, rocky body in orbit around the sun.

eclipse   the darkening of a heavenly body. It occurs when the shadow of one object in space falls on another object or when one object moves in front of another to block the light given off by the object.

epicycle   according to ancient astronomers, the circular shape that a planet was said to follow in its orbit. The center of an epicycle moves along a larger circle called a *deferent*.

exoplanet   a planet that orbits a star outside the solar system.

galaxy   a vast system of gas, dust, and stars held together in space by gravity.

Kuiper belt   a band of objects, known as **KBO's,** in the outer regions of our solar system, beyond the orbit of Neptune.

Main Belt   the region of our solar system located roughly between the orbits of the planets Mars and Jupiter. It is occupied by numerous asteroids.

probe   a spacecraft that carries scientific equipment but no people.

pulsar   a object in space thought to be a rapidly rotating star. It emits powerful radiation that arrives on Earth in regular pulses.

radiation   the emission of energy in the form of waves or as moving particles.

retrograde motion   the apparent motion as seen from Earth of a planet moving from east to west, reverse from the actual direction.

rocket   an engine that pushes upward against the force of Earth's gravity. It carries people and tools into space.

rover   a small battery- or solar-powered vehicle that can roll along the ground and perform tests using scientific tools.

solar system   the sun, its planets, and all other bodies that orbit the sun.

space shuttle   a rocket-launched spacecraft used to make repeated journeys between Earth and space.

supernova   a star that suddenly increases in brightness because of a huge explosion.

Find Out More

Books

Beyond the Solar System: Exploring Galaxies, Black Holes, Alien Planets, and More: A History with 21 Activities by Mary Kay Carson (Chicago Review Press, 2013)

The Kingfisher Space Encyclopedia by Mike Goldsmith (Kingfisher, 2012)

The Mighty Mars Rover: The Incredible Adventures of Spirit and Opportunity by Elizabeth Rusch (Houghton Mifflin Books for Children, 2012)

The Space Book: From the Beginning to the End of Time, 250 Milestones in the History of Space & Astronomy by Jim Bell (Sterling, 2013)

Space Encyclopedia: A Tour of Our Solar System and Beyond by David A. Aguilar (National Geographic Kids, 2013)

Space, Stars, and the Beginning of Time: What the Hubble Telescope Saw by Elaine Scott (Clarion Books, 2011)

Team Moon: How 400,000 People Landed Apollo 11 on the Moon by Catherine Thimmesh (Houghton Mifflin Harcourt, 2006)

Universe by Robin Kerrod (DK, 2015)

Websites

BBC Exploration
http://www.bbc.co.uk/science/space/universe/exploration
Watch dozens of videos on space exploration devices that attempt to answer the mysteries of the night sky.

HubbleSite
http://hubblesite.org/
Read blogs, watch videos, and view stunning images of space at NASA's official website for the Hubble Space Telescope.

NASA
https://www.nasa.gov/
Explore the website of NASA, which contains information about the space program's history, ongoing missions, and plans for the future.

National Geographic – Exploration Timelines
http://www.nationalgeographic.com/125/timelines/space-exploration/
See historical photos and artifacts while interacting with a clickable timeline of space flight.

Nova Space + Flight
http://www.pbs.org/wgbh/nova/space/
Take an in-depth look at astronomy and space exploration while reading articles, watching videos, and listening to podcasts.

Space.com
http://www.space.com/
Get the latest news about such space science topics as skywatching and the search for life in outer space.

Index